JIM ABBOTT
AGAINST ALL ODDS

Ellen Emerson White

SCHOLASTIC INC.
New York Toronto London Auckland Sydney

Photo Credits

Cover photo: © Ron Vesely/FOS
All Rights Reserved

ISBN 0-590-43503-5

12 11 10 9 8 7 6 5 4 3 2 1   0 1 2 3 4 5/9

Printed in the U.S.A.   28

First Scholastic printing, April 1990

Acknowledgments

I would like to thank everybody who helped me with this book. My particular thanks go to Jim Abbott; Jim Samia, Dick Bresciani, and the Boston Red Sox; Tim Mead and the California Angels; Mark Marquess; Bob Holec; Dave Cunningham; Regina Griffin; and Sarah White.

JIM ABBOTT
AGAINST ALL ODDS

It is a clear summer night at famous Fenway Park in Boston, and a rookie has come to town. He is tall, and strong, and young.

The California Angels, his team, is in a hot pennant race and tonight they need a win from their rookie pitcher. But he is facing the Boston Red Sox, the best hitting team in the American League.

The old green stadium is overflowing with die-hard Red Sox fans as the rookie takes the mound. *Noisy* die-hard Red Sox fans. But the rookie knows that he has to ignore the crowd — that he has to concentrate on tonight's game.

The rookie has an easy first two innings, but then, the Red Sox load the bases in the third. There are two outs, and the cleanup hitter, Mike Greenwell, strides to the plate. The crowd claps and cheers, begging their slugger to get a big hit.

The rookie takes a deep breath. The hitter waits, his bat up and ready. And the rookie strikes him out with his best fastball.

As the game goes on, the rookie strikes out more Red Sox hitters. Star first baseman Nick Esasky. Future Hall-of-Famer Dwight Evans. Rising star Ellis Burks. In the end, the rookie strikes out seven batters. He gives up four harmless hits and, most importantly, no runs.

When the rookie gets the final out of the game, giving his team a 4–0 victory, he starts to walk off the mound. All over Fenway Park, the Red Sox fans stand and applaud, cheering the rookie off the field. Their team may have lost, but they know that they have seen someone very special. That *this* is a pitcher.

This is Jim Abbott.

1
Growing Up

James Anthony Abbott was born on September 19, 1967, and has already led an eventful life. While attending the University of Michigan, he pitched his team to two Big Ten championships and was selected to the All-America team. Then, while playing in the Pan-American Games, he helped Team USA win the silver medal. Later, as a pitcher for the 1988 Olympic team, Jim was on the mound when the United States won the gold medal. Finally, Jim was picked by the California Angels in the major league baseball draft, becoming only the fifteenth player in the history of the draft to go straight to the big leagues without ever spending a day in the minors.

What makes all of this even more remarkable is that Jim Abbott has only one hand.

Born with a normal left arm, Jim has a right arm that is normal, too — except that it stops at the wrist. But from the time he was a small child, no one ever told Jim that he was handicapped, and he never acted that way. In fact, Jim was always about as far from handicapped as it was possible to be.

Jim was born and grew up in Flint, Michigan. His parents, Mike and Kathy Abbott, married very young and had to work hard to make ends meet. Jim's father is now a sales manager, and his mother is an attorney. She works for a law firm that focuses on educational issues. Education was always very important to the Abbotts.

"My parents always stressed school," Jim says now. "They wanted me to do well. They always said that I thought of sports first, but they made me think not just about baseball, but about getting good grades."

When Jim first went to school, a doctor fitted him with an artificial right hand, which had metal hooks on the end that he could clamp together to pick things up. But Jim never liked this fake, mechanical hand. By the time he was six, he had stopped wearing it completely.

Jim's parents always told him that he could do anything he wanted to do. They knew that their son loved sports. They hoped that Jim would play soccer — one of the few sports where he wouldn't need two hands — but right from the very beginning, Jim loved baseball. So, Jim's parents bought him a baseball glove. As it turned out, Jim's brother Chad was the one who liked soccer.

Now that he had a baseball glove, Jim had to learn how to throw — and catch — with the same hand. With his father's help, Jim developed what is now known as his famous glove switch. What he does is very complicated, but *looks* very easy. In fact, people often watch him play without even noticing that he is doing it all with just one hand.

As Jim throws the ball, he bends his right arm up in front of him and balances his glove on the end of it. Then, after he releases the ball, he slides his left hand into his glove. By the time the ball is batted or thrown back at him, he is ready to catch it. To watch Jim, it seems so easy. But, as is true for every great athlete, he practiced for many hours to perfect this.

Jim would practice this glove switch by playing catch with his father, and by throwing a ball against the side of his house and catching it as it bounced off. He would move closer and closer to the house, throwing the ball harder and harder, and getting better and faster with the glove switch. Today, he is able to pitch the ball and get the glove onto his hand before the ball even gets to home plate.

After Jim catches the ball, he moves his glove up under his right arm, pulls his left hand out, and grabs the ball to throw it — all in one quick motion. And he almost never makes an error.

The very first game Jim pitched in Little League

was a no-hitter. His team, Lydia Simon Real Estate, scored so many runs that the game was stopped after only five innings. Word quickly got around that there was a pitcher in Flint, Michigan, who was better with one hand than most other pitchers were with two. For the first time, Jim was interviewed by reporters. He has had to deal with almost constant attention from reporters ever since.

Jim went on to pitch for Flint Central High School. He already had a very good fastball, but very few people believed that he would be able to field his position against more difficult competition. One high school team tested his fielding during his freshman year by having eight batters in a row bunt. The first hitter *did* get to first base safely, but Jim threw the next seven out. After that, teams didn't bunt against Jim very often.

"He was a tough kid, very competitive," Bob Holec, Jim's high school baseball coach, said. "You don't see too many like him. He was just a great kid. He was also very successful socially and academically. He had a lot of friends."

By the time Jim was a senior, he was pitching and playing first base. He also spent some time in the outfield and even played shortstop briefly. He pitched four no-hitters that year and had an incredible 179 strikeouts in only eighty innings. That averages out to *more* than 2 strikeouts per inning. Over the length of the season, he gave up fewer than two hits a game.

6

Jim was also a very good hitter. He would hold the bat in his left hand, bracing the handle against his right wrist. Using this technique, he batted .427 his senior year, with seven home runs and thirty-six RBIs. He hit more home runs than anyone else on his team that year.

But there was more to Jim than just baseball. He was the top scorer in his school's intramural basketball league, and he played two years of varsity football. He was a punter, averaging thirty-seven-and-a-half yards per punt his senior year, and he was one of the team's quarterbacks.

Baseball coach Bob Holec is also one of the high school's football coaches. "I'll never forget this one game," he said, recalling one of the best punts Jim ever made. "Jim got a bad snap that went over his head, and he jumped up, snagged it with his one hand, and got the punt off. There were plenty of *oohs* and *aahs* from the crowd on *that* one." In fact, the whole time he played football, Jim never dropped a snap.

Then, late in the football season, when the starting quarterback became ineligible, Jim took over. He helped the Flint Central team get to the state play-offs, where they lost in the semifinals to the team that eventually won the state championship.

"He took a beating in that semifinal game," Coach Holec said, "but he still managed to get off four touchdown passes. He really came into his own at the end of the football season. You wish you had more like him."

Jim's various athletic exploits resulted in more press attention than ever, and Coach Holec was particularly impressed by the way Jim handled the reporters.

"He's a very humble person," Coach Holec explained. "There was never any jealousy from his teammates. A lot of kids would get big-headed from all of the attention, but Jim never did. He always praised his teammates, never himself." Then Coach Holec paused. "I would give him the finest compliment of all — if I had a son, I'd like him to be like Jim Abbott."

Jim had fun in high school, but he also studied, earning good grades. History was his favorite subject.

"I didn't like math much," Jim admits now, with a grin. "But I liked history and English — creative kinds of things. Art. Science, too."

After Jim graduated, the Toronto Blue Jays drafted him in the thirty-sixth round of the baseball draft and offered him a professional contract. Although Jim's dream was to play major league baseball, he wanted to continue his education, so he accepted a baseball scholarship to the University of Michigan. He would go to college first and hope that the major leagues would still be waiting when he was finished.

2
College Days

Once Jim got to college, he picked up right where he had left off in high school. His two main goals were to get an education and to become the best possible pitcher he could be. Of course, there would be nothing wrong with enjoying himself, too.

Early in Jim's college career, he decided that he would major in communications. Considering the amount of time he had spent surrounded by journalists, he certainly had a head start.

It was possible that Jim would be losing time in his professional baseball career, as a result of his decision to go to college. There aren't any minor leagues for professional football and basketball, so those sports recruit almost exclusively from college programs. A football or basketball player seeking an advantage would choose a university with a well-known and respected sports program. But baseball is different.

It takes a long time for a baseball player — especially a pitcher — to develop. It is not uncommon for a baseball player to spend four or five or even six years in the minors before moving up to the major leagues. Therefore, a player who signs a professional contract after graduating from high school is under much less pressure. He can take his time, moving up through the various levels of the minor leagues as he progresses. But a player who signs a contract after graduating from college is four years older, and if it takes him a few years in the minors, he will be in his mid-twenties by the time he gets to the big leagues. At that point, many players are at the peak of their careers. A player who goes to college first risks shortening his professional career.

On the other hand, for almost everyone, it is a more mature and sensible choice to go to college first. The odds against making it all the way to the big leagues are very high. After all, since there are twenty-six major league baseball teams — each of which has 24 players on its roster — there are only 624 major league baseball players at any given time. Out of all the millions of people who play baseball and would like to play professionally, 624 is a very small number. This means that, for every million people who want to play major league baseball, each person has only a 1600 to 1 chance of making it. Those are pretty slim odds.

Even if a player *does* make it to the big leagues, the possibility of getting injured is always there. An athlete who doesn't plan ahead — decide what to do once he or she can't play professional sports anymore — can end up regretting the decision not to go to college and get a degree. An educated athlete always has something to fall back on.

These were probably some of the things that Jim and his parents discussed when the Toronto Blue Jays offered him a contract. Jim made the wise decision to pursue his education *and* his baseball.

The University of Michigan coach Bud Middaugh is well known for his ability to help players improve, and Jim wanted to work on every aspect of his game.

At this point, his fastball was close to ninety miles per hour, and his slider was pretty good, too. Jim also wanted to work on a straight change-up and a better curveball.

Although there are a lot of articles about "fancier" pitches like split-fingered fastballs, forkballs, knuckleballs, and screwballs, it is a much better idea to stick to the basics. Anyone who can throw a ninety-mile-per-hour fastball, like Jim, doesn't need to fool around with those types of pitches. And even a pitcher who *can't* throw that hard would be better off working on control. A pitcher who can make the ball go anywhere he wants doesn't need to throw anything tricky. The secret to pitching is to throw the ball where the batter doesn't expect it, *when* the batter doesn't expect it. And Jim has spent many hours working on his control.

The fastball is the easiest pitch to throw. As long as the pitcher uses the proper form, the speed will come naturally. The fastball is thrown overhand, with your top two fingers going across the stitched seams, and your thumb underneath. It is important to put your whole body into the throw so that no unnecessary stress is put on your arm. Most pitchers believe that the way you use your legs to push forward is where the speed comes from — not from your arm. That is why pitchers use a windup. That way, your entire body moves smoothly, and your legs are naturally in position for the final drive forward. The fastball is Jim's best pitch.

Jim's next best pitch is his slider, or "cut fastball." The slider is thrown with a slightly different grip. To throw a slider, you hold your hand and wrist exactly the way you would if you were going to throw a tight spiral football pass. This grip will feel strange, at first, on a baseball, but with practice the slider is a very effective pitch.

Many baseball coaches believe that a pitcher shouldn't throw any breaking pitches — sliders, curveballs, and the like — until the player is fifteen or sixteen and has a fully mature arm. This is very good advice and prevents many injuries. When a slider is thrown properly, it *looks* like a fastball, but will move away from the batter, or into the batter (depending on whether the pitcher is left-handed or right-handed) at the last second. When he was younger, Jim spent most of his time working on his fastball, not breaking pitches.

One of the things Jim wanted to do while he was playing in college was to improve his curveball. To throw a curveball, a pitcher will cock his wrist to the side, and then snap it forward right before he releases the ball. This puts spin on the ball, causing it to curve. Professional baseball players are able to put different sorts of spin on the ball, allowing them to add more than one kind of breaking pitch to their repertoire. A breaking pitch is a pitch that moves or curves.

The other pitch Jim wanted to work on was a change-up. A change-up is thrown exactly the way you would throw a fastball, except that you don't throw it as hard. The batter expects to see a fastball, so he swings early, and misses the pitch. Since a lot of batters are able to guess *where* a pitcher is going to throw a pitch, good pitchers learn to throw at different speeds so that they can destroy the batter's timing.

Jim's freshman baseball season at Michigan was very successful. His very first victory came against North Carolina. Although Jim had always been — and still is — a starting pitcher, in this particular game, he came in as a relief pitcher. It was the seventh inning, and there were two outs, with a North Carolina runner on third. Planning to take advantage of the fact that Jim had to switch his glove to his left hand when the catcher threw the ball back to him, the runner tried to steal home. Without batting an eye, Jim threw the runner out to end the inning.

Later in the game, the Michigan Wolverines took the lead, and Jim had his first college victory.

Jim won six games and lost only two his freshman year. One of his victories was the game that allowed his team to clinch the Big Ten championship against the University of Minnesota. (Colleges are organized into various conferences — or divisions — and Michigan is a member of the Big Ten Conference.)

Jim pitched just over fifty innings that season and had forty-four strikeouts. He also had a 4.11 earned run average. A pitcher's earned run average is figured out by multiplying the number of earned runs the pitcher has allowed the other team to score, by nine, and then dividing *that* number by the number of innings the pitcher has pitched. A 4.00 earned run average is quite good, and an earned run average that is 3.00 or below is excellent. A 3.00 earned run average means that the pitcher has allowed the other team to score only three runs in every nine-inning game. Any manager would be pleased to have a pitcher who could consistently do that.

After Michigan won the Big Ten championship,

Jim received the honor of being selected to the Big Ten Play-offs All-Tournament team — as a freshman. Earlier that season, the national sports cable network, ESPN, chose Jim as their "Amateur Athlete of the Week." This was after Jim pitched a sparkling 1–0 game against Western Michigan State.

All in all, Jim had every reason to be very pleased by his first year in college baseball.

Jim's sophomore season was even better. In fifteen starts, Jim posted eleven wins against only three losses. He pitched three shutouts that season and had one thirty-one-inning stretch during which he didn't give up any runs at all. That streak, and the three shutouts, resulted in Jim's brilliant 2.03 earned run average for the season, and he pitched more than eighty-five innings for the team.

After losing his first game of the season, Jim won the next nine straight. He had nine strikeouts in one game. And, just in case anyone still had any doubts about his ability to field the ball, it is worth mentioning that Jim had only three errors — total — in his first two seasons at Michigan. That would be good for any pitcher — especially one with only one hand.

The Michigan Wolverines — helped a great deal by Jim's pitching — won the Big Ten championship for the second year in a row, and Jim was named to the All-Big Ten second team. He was also selected as a third-team All-America. Jim pitched a 10–0 shutout against New Jersey's Rider

College in the NCAA tournament, and more than one professional baseball scout showed up to see him pitch. In his first two seasons at Michigan, Jim hadn't done *anything* to hurt his chances of becoming a professional baseball player. If anything, he had improved them.

3
The Pan-American Games

Later in 1987, Jim received the greatest honor so far in his pitching career: He was chosen to represent the United States on the national team that would be playing in the Pan-American Games. The Pan-American Games are very much like the Olympics, except that only countries from North, South, and Central America are eligible to compete. In 1987, the Games were to be held in Indianapolis, Indiana.

The head baseball coach for the United States baseball team was Ron Fraser, from the University of Miami. The best amateur baseball players in the country — mostly college players — were chosen to be on the team. These players included Ty Griffin, a switch-hitting second baseman from Georgia Tech; Gregg Olson, a pitcher from Auburn

University; Tino Martinez, a first baseman from Tampa University; and Ted Wood, a left fielder from the University of New Orleans.

The Pan-American Games were set to begin in early August, and once the US team — known as Team USA — had been assembled, and practiced together, they set off on a pre-Games tour to get ready. The highlight of the tour was the team's trip to Havana, Cuba, in mid-July. The Cuban baseball team has dominated Pan-American competition for over twenty years.

The United States and Cuba have many political and diplomatic differences, but baseball is Cuba's most popular sport. It is said that their leader, Fidel Castro — who went to more than one major league baseball tryout as a young man, but was never signed to a contract — would never have *become* a leader if he had ever managed to make it onto an American big league team. There may be more legend than truth to this story, but it is a very interesting theory. Either way, Fidel Castro loves baseball. He especially likes pitchers, since that is what he had hoped to be.

Gregg Olson, a Team USA pitcher who was Jim's roommate throughout the summer, described the trip to Havana this way: "Well, it was a good experience," he said. "Not too many people have ever been down there. They don't really want Americans down there, except for athletes. But just the experience of playing the Cubans at their place was worth everything that we went through."

Team USA was to play five games against the Cuban team, and Jim was slated to start the first one. More than 50,000 fans were there to watch the game, and Fidel Castro came down personally to meet Jim and shake his hand.

Jim won the game, and he won the fans, too, when the first batter hit the ball to him and Jim fielded it bare-handed to throw the runner out. The crowd went wild. During the entire time that Team USA was in Cuba, people would follow Jim through the streets, wanting to get a look at him.

"It was fun," Gregg Olson remembered. "We beat them two out of five. Jim pitched the first one, and I pitched the second one that we won."

By the time the thirty-four-game pre-Games tour was over, Jim had won six games and lost only one, and he was more than ready for the real Games to begin.

The Pan-American Games are played every four years, the year before the Olympics. In many ways, they serve as a rehearsal for athletes expecting to compete in the Olympics.

When the Games opened in Indianapolis, there were more than 80,000 people present to watch the opening ceremonies. Thirty-eight countries were represented, with more than 6,000 athletes, who would be competing in twenty-seven different sports. Other than baseball, some of the sports included were track and field, basketball, diving, gymnastics, swimming, field hockey, judo, soccer, softball, swimming, weight lifting, and cycling.

Many of the athletes were housed in dormitories at nearby Fort Benjamin, while others were placed in Indianapolis motels.

Then Vice President George Bush presided over the opening ceremonies. Former basketball star Oscar Robertson and former track star Wilma Rudolph were involved in the ceremonial lighting of the Pan-American Games torch.

The United States delegation was comprised of 667 athletes. Only one could be chosen to lead the delegation and carry the American flag.

It was very hard to choose among so many great athletes, but finally, the choice was narrowed to Jim, basketball player David Robinson, and diver Greg Louganis. Jim was thrilled when he was the one chosen — out of all those talented people — to head the American delegation.

The United States delegation was snappily dressed in matching white tropical suits, with red suspenders and Panama fedoras. Proudly, Jim marched at the front of the pack, holding the American flag.

And so, the Games began.

Team USA's game uniforms were red, white, and blue. Their pants were white, with red and blue trim, and they would wear either dark blue or white shirts. Jim wore uniform number thirty-eight.

The last time the Pan-American Games had been held in the United States was in Chicago, in 1959. It was exciting for Jim and his teammates to be able to play for the United States, *in* the United States.

Team USA won their first two games — against Canada and Venezuela — and Jim was to pitch their third game, against Nicaragua. Although Team USA was playing well, the Cuban team was still favored to win the gold medal. Team USA had every intention of preventing that from happening. One reason why the Americans were the underdog was that Team USA was made up of almost all young college players, while many of their opponents' teams — like Cuba's — were made up of athletes who were eight or ten years older and major-league-caliber players.

The first batter Jim faced in the game against Nicaragua laid down a bunt, hoping that Jim would make an error. Jim fielded it without any trouble and had a very easy inning. Then his teammates scored ten runs in the bottom half of the first inning, and the slaughter was on.

Jim pitched five shutout innings, giving up only four hits, while walking four and striking out six of the Nicaraguan batters. Coach Ron Fraser, who preferred to be careful with his young pitchers and not let them pitch too long, then took Jim out of the game and let another pitcher finish up. Because of the high score, the game was called after seven innings.

The final score of the game was an embarrassing 18–0, in favor of the United States. In their first three games, Team USA — supposedly a weak-hitting team — scored a total of forty-two runs, for an average of fourteen per game. So far, they were not being challenged.

A couple of days later, they *did* face a challenge: Cuba. The last time Cuba had lost a game in official Pan-American competition was when they lost to the United States in 1967. That was the only year that the United States ever won the gold medal in baseball in the Pan-Am Games. Cuba had had an impressive thirty-three-game winning streak going ever since.

Team USA changed all of that. Second baseman Ty Griffin hit two home runs, and pitchers Chris Nichting and Jim Poole combined to pitch a very good game. The score was tied, 4–4, in the bottom of the ninth, when Ty Griffin stepped up to the plate. There were two outs. With one dramatic swing, Ty hit his second home run of the game, and Team USA shattered Cuba's twenty-year Pan-American winning streak. It was one of the most exciting moments during the entire 1987 Pan-Am competition.

Team USA continued to win, but so did Cuba. It was inevitable that the two teams would meet in the final for the gold medal. Team USA beat Puerto Rico in a tense eleven-inning game, behind Cris Carpenter's fine pitching. Then, thanks to Jim — and Cris Carpenter's relief work — the team beat Canada. Now Cuba was the only team between them and the gold medal.

The gold medal game was a very bizarre game. Gregg Olson was the starting pitcher. In the first inning, there was a rain delay, and the scoreboard was actually struck by lightning. By the time the game got underway again, both Gregg, and the Cuban pitcher Pablo Abrea, had lost their rhythms, and it turned into a high-scoring game.

At one point, Team USA had an 8–5 lead, but when a tired Cris Carpenter came in in relief, he was unable to hold the lead. He pitched two very good innings, but the Cuban team came back strong in the eighth inning and ended up winning by a score of 13–9. Cuba hit a total of four home runs during the game.

Cuba went home with the gold medal, but after winning eight out of nine games, Jim and his teammates had to be pleased with their silver medal effort.

Jim pitched in three of the nine games and ended up with a two-win-and-no-loss record, with a mind-boggling *0.00* earned run average. His record for the summer, including the pre-Games tour, worked out to eight victories against only one loss. His earned run average was 1.70, and he had fifty-one strikeouts in just under forty-eight innings pitched. It would have been almost impossible for him to have pitched any better.

"You know," Gregg Olson said later, "everyone gets the impression that he's the all-American guy, and it's true. Everybody knows who he is, no matter where he goes, and I imagine that it's tough on him. But he handles the pressure. I hope he keeps it up — he's a good friend."

Jim had had such a great summer that it was hard to imagine that things could get even better. But they did.

4
A Dream Come True

In the fall of 1987, Jim was given the United States Baseball Federation's coveted Golden Spikes Award. This award is given to the best amateur baseball player in the country every year. It was the perfect finish to Jim's baseball year.

That wasn't the only award Jim got. He got the Academy Awards of Sport Award for Courage in 1987, and he was chosen as the March of Dimes Amateur Athlete of the Year for 1988. Then, he won the Tanqueray Achievement Award for amateur athletes. However, his biggest honor came in March 1988.

Every year, the Amateur Athletic Union gives out the prestigious Sullivan Award. This award is given to the best amateur athlete of the year — in *any* sport. In the fifty-eight-year history of the award, it had never been given to a baseball player.

The competition was very stiff. Basketball whiz David Robinson was a finalist for the award, as was Karch Kiraly, the star of the United States gold-medal-winning volleyball team. World hurdle champion Greg Foster was nominated, as were diver Greg Louganis, track star Jackie Joyner-Kersee, and swimmer Janet Evans. These were the best athletes in the entire country, and Jim would have felt honored just to be nominated. He was stunned when he won. It would be enough to make anyone's head spin. But Jim, as always, handled the situation with grace and good sportsmanship.

It was spring now, 1988, and his junior baseball season at Michigan lay ahead. Jim had another fantastic season. He won nine games, while losing only three. He pitched almost ninety innings, and had eighty-two strikeouts.

At one point during the season, he pitched two shutouts in a row. In that second shutout, he also struck out twelve batters — the most strikeouts he'd had in any game at Michigan.

Aware that the baseball draft was approaching, Jim's coach, Bud Middaugh, decided to try a little experiment. Knowing that Jim had been a very good hitter in high school, Coach Middaugh let him be the designated hitter during a game he wasn't pitching, so that the baseball scouts would be able to see him at the plate.

Jim — always one to rise to an occasion — got two hits. Any National League scouts who might have worried about drafting Jim, since pitchers *do* have to hit in the National League, would no longer worry about *that* aspect of Jim's game.

As the season came to an end, Jim once again led the Wolverines to the play-offs. This time, he was not only selected to the Big Ten Play-offs All-Tournament team, he was also named to the Big Ten 1st team. To top it off, he was chosen as the Big Ten Conference Player of the Year. Since it was likely that he would be drafted — somewhere — in the upcoming major league baseball draft, Jim knew that he had probably played his last college game. He certainly went out with a bang.

Over three college seasons, Jim had won twenty-six games and lost only eight. His final earned run average was 3.03. In forty-one starts, he had thirteen complete games. He had 186 strikeouts in just over 234 innings. He had six career shutouts. Finally, in three seasons, he made only three errors. He didn't make *any* errors in his junior season. He also, of course, had those two hits.

With all of these fine numbers behind him, it was time to wait for the baseball draft. He would need only a few more college credits to graduate, and he could complete them during the off-season. As a baseball player, he needed new challenges.

On draft day, Jim was the eighth pick in the first round. He was selected by the California Angels. He was the fifth pitcher to be chosen in the draft, and the second left-hander. The Angels were very happy to have him.

The very first pick in the draft was pitcher Andy Benes, who went to the San Diego Padres. The Baltimore Orioles, who had the fourth pick, chose Jim's Pan-American Games roommate, pitcher Gregg Olson. All told, in the first round, thirteen of the twenty-six picks (each major league team has one pick) were pitchers. Eighteen of the first twenty-six picks were college students, the highest number ever. This was yet another indication that Jim had made the right decision to spend some time in college instead of signing a contract after graduating from high school.

Many of Jim's former Pan-Am teammates were chosen in the draft. Ty Griffin went to the Cubs; first baseman Tino Martinez went to the Seattle Mariners. Pitcher Cris Carpenter was chosen by the St. Louis Cardinals, and pitcher Chris Nichting went to the Dodgers. By the time the draft was over, members of Team USA were well represented.

Around this same time, Jim was asked to represent the United States on the 1988 Olympic baseball team. He now had to make a decision. He could either sign with the Angels right away, and start his career in the minor leagues, or he could postpone signing in order to keep his amateur status and play in the Olympics. For Jim, the choice was easy — he wanted to play in the Olympics.

Some of his old teammates — Ty Griffin, Ted

Wood, Tino Martinez, and Scott Servais among others — made the same decision. Other old teammates, like Gregg Olson and Cris Carpenter, elected to begin their professional careers immediately.

Jim also made the decision to leave college without finishing his degree.

"Well, I have my three years," he said later, "and I'll see where that takes me. I geared myself somewhat towards other things, but I always hoped that baseball would be It. Hopefully, I'll get some more schooling while I'm still playing — maybe even finish up."

While Jim hadn't completed his studies, he knew that there wasn't much more he could accomplish in baseball at the college level. It was time to move on.

5
Olympic Gold

Baseball was a new sport for the Olympics — it had been a demonstration sport in 1984 and wouldn't be a full-fledged medal sport until 1992, but there was already a strong tradition of Olympic players going on to the major leagues. Members of the 1984 squad who are currently playing in the big leagues include Mark McGwire, Will Clark, Barry Larkin, B.J. Surhoff, and Cory Snyder. A total of thirteen players from the 1984 Olympic team have made it to the majors.

Ten of the first-round picks from the 1988 baseball draft were also chosen to be on the 1988 Olympic team. Nine played in the Olympics. The tenth first-round pick chosen, Gregg Olson, went on to his career with the Orioles.

The head coach of the 1988 Olympic baseball

team was Mark Marquess, the head baseball coach at Stanford University. He explained exactly how the Olympic baseball team is selected.

"The coaching staff is made up of about four coaches, normally coaches from throughout the United States," Coach Marquess said. "In the fall, they'll start talking about who the better amateur players are. Then the coaching staff gets to invite twenty-five players, and each division from within the amateur ranks — for example, Division Two or Division Three — gets to send three players. You cover all of amateur baseball so that everybody is represented.

"Then," Coach Marquess continued, "it ends up with about forty players. Millington, Tennessee, is our training site. So, my coaching staff selected twenty-five players — Jim obviously being one of them, since everyone knew how good he was — and then we had fifteen players from these other divisions. We worked out for a week or two, and then made cuts. We cut to twenty-five players. All of the international tournaments, including the Olympics, have twenty players, so right before the World Baseball Tournament in Italy, we had to cut it down again to twenty. Most of the time, there's a group of ten or twelve players everyone is pretty sure about — you know, Ty Griffin, Robin Ventura, Jim Abbott, Ben MacDonald, Andy Benes — everyone knows those guys are the best, and you want them. But when you get down to that last five or six, that's where the tryout comes into play. And professional baseball has been good; they've helped us out quite a bit. I would talk to a lot of pro scouts and they would say, well, so-and-so, you've got to invite him, and it really helped."

Once the team had been put together, they set off on a grueling three-month pre-Olympic tour. The team traveled over 30,000 miles on this tour, playing all over America, then in Japan, and then in Italy, at the World Baseball Tournament. After *that*, they would head on to Seoul, Korea, and the actual Olympics.

In August, the team played seven games with the Cuban national team in various parts of the southern United States. They also faced the Korean national team for five games in Tulsa, Oklahoma.

The tour was exhausting, as the team rarely spent two nights in one town — sometimes not even in one *country* — and never three nights in a row. Often, they would also be suffering from severe jet lag, and there were regular 4:15 A.M. wake-up calls. If nothing else, the team developed a lot of stamina over these long weeks. They also won their share of games.

"I mean, here you are," Coach Marquess said, "we had all these nineteen-, twenty-year-old kids, and there was never any problem, never any trouble." Then he laughed. "Of course, we traveled so much that they were so tired that they couldn't *get* in much trouble. But it was a special experience.

It's something that you'll never forget."

A lot of the players on the team had been on the Pan-American team, but there were some new faces, too, like Robin Ventura and Andy Benes. Cuba was boycotting the Olympics — although they defeated the United States in the World Baseball Championships in Italy right before the Olympics — and the United States team's biggest rivals in the Olympic Games would be 1984-defending-champion Japan, Taiwan, and South Korea.

Jim pitched extremely well during the pre-Games tour, compiling an eight-win record against only one defeat, with an earned run average of 2.55. As usual, he was surpassing everyone's expectations.

"One thing about Jim is that he always seems to pitch well in big games. The times when Jim wouldn't pitch as well were — well, just games. Every *big* game we had, he pitched super," Coach Marquess said later.

By the time the Olympic Games opened, the baseball team was a strong, cohesive — and tired — unit.

"Jim is one of the guys," Coach Marquess said. "He fits in well. On the Olympic team, he got all of the publicity, and when that happens, other players have a tendency to resent it. But they didn't. They loved him, because of the type of person that he was. I think that says it all about Jim Abbott, when you're more impressed by him as a person than you are as an athlete."

The glare of publicity was constant for Jim, and often very demanding.

"Many times, he'll speak to young handicapped kids, and *not* for publicity," Coach Marquess remembered. "In Japan, all the newspaper and television people were trying to get interviews with him, and one of the TV people said, we would like you to speak to a young boy who has only one hand. And Jim said, 'I would be happy to do that, but I don't want to do it in front of the television cameras.' And the people just walked away, because they were only using it as a gimmick to get him on television. Jim would do anything to help anyone else, but he's not out to get publicity. In fact, he shies away from it."

When the 1988 Summer Olympic Games finally got underway, there were almost 10,000 athletes participating. Jim celebrated his twenty-first birthday during the Games. He found it very exciting to walk around the Olympic Village, and meet so many talented and famous athletes from all of the various sports. He especially enjoyed meeting tennis players like Pam Shriver and Gabriella Sabatini.

Jim made his inaugural Olympic appearance in a game against Canada. He pitched three innings, and while his control was a little off, he got seven strikeouts. He gave up four singles, and after Coach Marquess felt that he had had a good workout, he took Jim out of the game. He would need Jim to be rested and strong for the medal round.

The team wore gray uniforms with red, white, and blue trim. Their hats were blue, with a USA logo on the front, and a red bill. This time, Jim's number was thirty-one.

It was only fitting, really, that the United States went up against the defending champions, Japan, in the final game. The winner of the game would get the gold medal. In picking his pitcher for this game, Coach Marquess had an easy choice.

"When it was the biggest game of the whole tour — the reason we'd all been together for four months — Jim was the guy that I picked," he said.

The game was played in Chamshil Baseball Stadium, in front of a good-sized crowd. Jim and his teammates had worked so hard for so many weeks, and now it all came down to this one contest.

"We were to the point where our starting pitchers — especially in the big games — had to go almost the whole way, and Jim knew that," Coach Marquess explained, since the long pre-Games tour had exhausted the pitching staff more than anyone else. "So that put a little more pressure on him."

Jim pitched very well until the sixth inning, when he walked in a run. But Coach Marquess and the rest of his staff decided to stick with him. Jim got the next two batters to ground out, although one more run scored, and the United States was out of the inning with a thin one-run lead.

Jim knew that everyone was counting on him to

finish the game, so he went back out to pitch the last three innings. First baseman Tino Martinez — who was having a fantastic day at the plate — hit a solo home run in the eighth inning to give the United States a 5–3 lead. Now all Jim had to do was hold it.

"You know, he lost a real difficult game in Italy," Coach Marquess remembered. "We played Cuba for the gold medal in that tournament, and we had a bad call at first base. The next thing you know, they've tied it, and they beat us after we'd had a two-run lead in the ninth. Now, we have a two-run lead in the Olympics, in the ninth inning, and you know that's in the back of his mind."

Jim rose to the challenge like a true champion. He got the Japanese batters to hit three straight ground balls — all of which went to third baseman Robin Ventura — and the game was over. The United States had won the gold medal!

The entire team ran to the mound and jumped on Jim, and he found himself at the bottom of a large, happy pile of baseball players. The celebration continued as the rest of the team took a victory lap around the field and Jim, tired, but very happy, stood on the mound, watching them. It was yet another magic moment in his baseball career.

"People always ask what Jim Abbott is *really* like," Coach Marquess reflected, much later, "because most of the time, the all-American image isn't really true. But he *is* the *true* all-American boy, both on and off the field. You have to give a lot of credit to his parents — they're special people. They had to have had a difficult decision. Because when you're young, and you're playing sports, the kids make fun of you if you screw up. I don't care if you have one hand or two — that's just the way they are. I've always admired Jim's parents for letting him go ahead and do those things. I mean, all of us have days when we say, gee, I don't think I can do this, and we have a defeatist attitude, and here's this guy, with just the one hand, who does *everything*. He is really very special. I think that it gives everyone else hope. It's quite a story. Not just for young people, but for everybody. And it's not just a baseball story. You don't have to know anything about athletics to appreciate Jim Abbott. Simply because of what he's done, what he's overcome. You can't say enough good things about him."

Now that the Olympics were over, Jim's next step would be to begin his professional career as a member of the California Angels' organization. There would be a lot of new challenges ahead. For one thing, Jim had never pitched to a batter using a wooden bat before; he had always pitched to hitters using aluminum bats. He would have to learn some new strategies and techniques.

Jim knew that he would be ready to give his new career everything he had — and he could hardly wait to get started.

6
Spring Training

In spring training, it is generally assumed that the higher the number a player is assigned, the less chance he has of making the team. For example, a player who is given, say, number five, is a player the major league club is very excited about, and expects to make the team, or at least to make the Triple-A farm club. When Jim got to the California Angels' spring training camp in late February, the number on his uniform was sixty.

The Angels were planning to assign Jim to their Double-A farm club in Midland, Texas. Down there, they figured, he would be able to get some experience, and maybe in a couple of years he would be ready to try to play at the major league level. But Jim had different plans.

Most major league baseball teams have very extensive minor league systems. There are several playing levels, the highest being Triple-A. The other levels — going down in order — are Double-A, Single-A, and the Rookie (or Instructional) League. Most young players who are signed to professional contracts start off in the Instructional League (a league that also used to be known as Class-B, Class-C, or even Class-D). Then, they work their way up to the major leagues, a step at a time. Many of them, of course, never make it. Many players, in fact, don't even make it as high as the Triple-A farm club, one step below the majors.

Because of all this, it was a great compliment to Jim that the Angels wanted to start him as high as their Double-A club, the Midland Angels. But Jim was confident that if he worked as hard as he could, he would be able to *start* in the major leagues. So, he went into spring training with that idea in mind.

Very few athletes in history have made it to the professional level in *any* sport with a physical handicap, and because of this, many people doubted that Jim would really be able to do it. But Jim knew that he had always had to prove himself before, and he was ready to do it again.

There was a man named Pete Gray, who played outfield for the Saint Louis Browns baseball team back in 1945. Pete had only one arm, but he was still able to hit .218 at the major league level. Unfortunately that wasn't good enough for him to have a long-term professional career, and 1945 was the only year that he played in the big leagues.

In the 1930s, the Chicago White Sox had a star pitcher named Monty Stratton. In 1937, he went 15–5, with a 2.40 earned run average. He was a young man, and the White Sox expected to have him around for a long time. Monty won another fifteen games the next year, but then was in a tragic accident and lost one of his legs. Monty made a brave try at a comeback and was somewhat successful, but he was never able to pitch as well as he had before the accident.

There was also a pitcher named Mordecai Brown, who pitched in the early part of this century. Mordecai's nickname was "Three Finger" Brown, because he had only three fingers on his pitching hand. He was a star pitcher for the Chicago Cubs team that featured the famous "Tinker-to-Evers-to-Chance" double-play combination. Three Finger Brown won 239 games in his career and struck out almost 1400 batters. He is now in the Hall of Fame.

Finally, although the rules of baseball were slightly different in those days (for example, it took five balls to get a walk to first base, instead of four), a one-armed pitcher named Hugh Daily struck out 19 batters in one game in 1887.

So, if Jim could make the big league team, he would be the first player in many, many years to overcome such odds.

The first game Jim pitched in spring training was a "B-Squad" exhibition game against the

Jim Abbott relies on his now famous glove-switch so he can pitch and field with the same hand.

Jim was already a stand-out pitcher during his years at Flint Central High School in Michigan.

*While pitching for the University of Michigan Wolverines,
Jim Abbott led them to two Big Ten championships.*

In 1987 Jim pitched for the U.S. at the Pan-American Games. Team USA brought home the silver medal.

Padres B-Squad on March 3, 1989. Spring training camps divide their players into A-Squads and B-Squads, with B-Squad players expected to end up in the minors.

Well, eight of Jim's first nine pitches were strikes. He had made an excellent beginning. In three innings, he gave up two hits, no runs, no walks, and he struck out four Padres. There were so many reporters around that Jim was forced to hold a press conference — the first of many during spring training — to answer questions.

The Angels were very impressed by their young pitcher's debut and decided to have him pitch an A-Squad game a few days later against the Oakland Athletics. With two outs, and men on second and third, José Canseco came up to the plate. With first base open, Jim could have walked Canseco — a feared home-run hitter — but Jim decided to pitch to him. And, in this first major confrontation of his professional career, Jim was the winner. He struck out Canseco on a very nasty slider.

Now, people were really starting to sit up and take notice of Jim. His control was a little wild — he had walked the two hitters who were on base when Canseco came to the plate — but the Angels were impressed by Jim's confidence and maturity, and also by his slider.

At this stage, Jim was throwing his fastball and a slider, but the Angels were also having him work to improve his curveball and develop a better change-up.

"He's basically a two-pitch pitcher right now," Marcel Lachemann, the Angels' pitching coach, said. "Fastball and slider. It is an above-average major league fastball. The average major league fastball on the JUGS gun" — which is a kind of radar gun, designed specifically for baseball — "is eighty-eight to ninety miles an hour, and he's consistently at ninety-two to ninety-three." The highest speed at which Jim has registered on the Angels' radar gun — so far — is ninety-four miles an hour. *That* is a very good fastball.

Although Jim was embarrassed by the fact that, as a mere rookie, he was constantly surrounded by the press, as spring training went on his performances were more and more impressive.

Jim got his first victory against the Milwaukee Brewers with three very good innings of middle relief. Increasingly the Angels' coaching staff was realizing that Jim was too good to start with the Double-A farm club. Now, the plan was for him to start at Triple-A, playing for the Edmonton Trappers, the best team in the Angels' minor league system.

Jim continued to pitch well. *Very* well. And the Angels — like all major league teams — needed left-handed pitchers. It began to seem more and more likely that Jim just might do the impossible: begin his career at the major league level.

Dave Cunningham, a reporter for the Long Beach *Press-Telegram* who covers the California Angels regularly, remembers it this way: "I was looking at him and saying, 'This guy's throwing as well as anyone in camp right now, and he's a rookie; is there a chance that he's going to stick with the big league club?' And they" — meaning the Angels' coaching staff — "said that with that slider that he can throw right at the knees, time after time, that he was as good as anyone on the club. They said they didn't know how they could keep him off, how they could possibly send him to the minor leagues."

According to Dave Cunningham, at that point, the Angels felt that Jim was definitely one of their top five pitchers in camp, if not one of the top two or three. "That was before they knew that Blyleven was going to come back with the great year," Dave explained, "and before they knew McCaskill was going to bounce back from the injuries. Right now, Jim's legitimately the number-five pitcher on the staff, and that's some achievement for a rookie."

But the decision still had not been made officially. For one thing, the Angels already *had* a fifth starting pitcher in Dan Petry. What made this ironic was that Dan Petry had played for the Detroit Tigers for many years. Growing up near Detroit, in Flint, Jim had always rooted for the Detroit Tigers. In fact, he had been a big fan of Dan Petry's. Now they were competing for the same position.

As it turned out, Dan Petry's shoulder was hurting him and he wasn't pitching very well, so Angel manager Doug Rader decided that Jim would be his fifth starter behind Mike Witt, Bert Blyleven, Kirk McCaskill, and Chuck Finley. Dan Petry made the team, but he would be a relief pitcher instead.

Jim, making a final spring training start against the San Diego Padres, pitched four good innings, and struck out Tony Gwynn. Tony had won the National League batting championship more than once, and it was the first time that *anyone* had gotten him to strike out during spring training that year.

And so, the decision was made. Jim would start the season as a member of the California Angels. What, exactly, was his new team like?

The Angels are owned by Gene Autry, the famous cowboy movie star. It is appropriate that a team located in Anaheim, California, near Disneyland and Hollywood, would have an owner like Gene Autry. Autry bought the team back in 1960, the year that the Angels were added to the major leagues. The Angels have had many famous players over the years — like Reggie Jackson, Don Baylor, and Nolan Ryan — but they have never gone to the World Series.

Nineteen eighty-nine was Angels' manager Doug Rader's first year with the team. He played major league baseball for eleven years, and was a fine fielding third baseman. Doug Rader had several coaches to help him, and Marcel Lachemann, who pitched for Oakland for three years, was his pitching coach.

The California Angels' pitching staff that Jim

joined was very strong. Bert Blyleven and Mike Witt were probably the two most experienced, while former hockey star Kirk McCaskill (who was offered professional contracts in both sports) and left-hander Chuck Finley were in the earlier stages of their careers. All four were very good pitchers. The bullpen pitchers included Bryan Harvey, Dan Petry, Willie Fraser, and Greg Minton.

On the field, the Angels had a good mix of veterans and young players. Their full-time catcher was dependable Lance Parrish, who also spent many years playing for the Detroit Tigers. It was exciting for Jim to be playing on the same team with Parrish. The designated hitter was another veteran, Brian Downing, who held most of the Angels' all-time hitting records.

The regular infield included young All-Star first baseman Wally Joyner, second baseman Johnny Ray, shortstops Dick Schofield and Kent Anderson, and third baseman Jack Howell.

The Angels' outfield was excellent. Claudell Washington, the underrated star who came over to the Angels from the Yankees, was the right fielder, while Devon White played center field, with Chili Davis in left. As it happens, Devon White and Chili Davis were *both* from Kingston, Jamaica, although they grew up in the United States and never met until they became teammates. These two athletes may also become big stars in the American League in the next few years.

Naturally the Angels had a lot of backup players,

in case someone got hurt, or went into a slump, or otherwise needed to be replaced in the lineup. These players included catcher Bill Schroeder, infielders Glenn Hoffman and Robert Rose, and outfielders Tony Armas and Dante Bichette.

This was Jim's new team. The Angels would be underdogs in the Western Division, with the powerful Oakland Athletics expected to repeat as 1989 division winners. But the Angels had the potential to be right in the middle of the pennant race. The most important key to the Angels' chances would be how their pitching staff performed. Part of that would be Jim's responsibility.

Jim handed in his uniform with the number sixty, and was given a new, permanent uniform bearing the number twenty-five. Finally, after all those years of dreaming, Jim was a major league baseball pitcher.

7
Opening Day

Now that Jim had made the team, the press *really* went wild. The amateur baseball draft had begun back in 1965, and Jim was only the fifteenth player in history to go directly from the draft to the big leagues. The most recent player to do so was Pete Incaviglia, an outfielder and first baseman with the Texas Rangers, who did it in 1985. Other players among the fifteen include pitcher Mike Morgan, former Atlanta third baseman Bob Horner, and New York Yankee outfielder Dave Winfield. Even stars like Bo Jackson, Roger Clemens, and Kirby Puckett all spent time in the minor leagues before coming up to the majors. Jim had achieved something very special.

Nine of the other fifteen players who came directly to the majors were pitchers. Only one of them, Burt Hooton, who pitched for the Cubs in 1971, had a winning record in their first year. The other eight had a combined nineteen victories and forty-four defeats in their first seasons. Dick Ruthven, who pitched for the Philadelphia Phillies in 1973, had the most victories his first year, with six. Even though Jim had now made the team, he still had some very challenging times ahead.

Right before spring training ended, the Angels held an intrasquad game, and had Jim pitch for the Triple-A Edmonton team against the regular Angels, to practice pitching against real major leaguers. Jim responded to the challenge. He pitched six innings against his future teammates, giving up only three singles as the Triple-A Trappers beat the parent club, 13–1. That gave Jim three wins and only one loss during spring training, and he finished camp with a 3.91 earned run average. The Angels' coaches, needless to say, were very pleased and excited about their new rookie pitcher.

On the day of Jim's first regular-season start, the field was crowded with reporters before the game.

"It was amazing," reporter Dave Cunningham said, remembering that day. "It was like the World Series, or a Super Bowl. Just a huge crush of people out there."

Angel pitching coach Marcel Lachemann agreed with this. "I think the thing that separates him from everyone else is the way that he's able to handle all of the media attention, plus all the normal publicity that *any* young kid is going to get," he said. "He handles everything probably as well as any veteran player I've ever seen."

During that first game, Jim — understandably — felt the pressure, and he didn't pitch very well. He was facing the Seattle Mariners and their ace, Mark Langston.

Jim gave up hits to the first two batters, and it was 2–0 by the end of the first inning — *against* the Angels. In the second inning, Jim set down the side in order. He ran into some trouble in the third, after an error by one of his teammates, a single, and a walk, but he got out of the inning with a double play. In the fifth inning, after there was another error behind him, Jim gave up four runs, and left the game, behind 6–0. The Angels ended up losing by the score of 7–0.

Of course, Jim was disappointed, but because of the errors, three of the six runs he gave up had been unearned (which means that the pitcher is not considered responsible for those runs scoring). He had given up six hits and walked three batters, without getting any strikeouts.

Jim had thrown eighty-three pitches, forty-seven of which were strikes. The radar gun showed that his fastball got as high as ninety-four miles per hour during the game.

Alvin Davis, the excellent Mariner first baseman, was very impressed, although it had been his broken-bat single that drove Jim from the game. "He's got a good arm," Alvin said. "He's got two good pitches right now, and probably he'll develop a change-up as he gets a little more experience. But he's a good pitcher."

Mariner right fielder Jay Buhner agreed: "Just watching the way he handles himself, the way he goes about his business — he's such a hard worker," Jay observed. "I think he's going to be a great plus for the game, and I respect him for his courage. I think from here on out, you're going to see some other kids in the situation he's in, and it's a great, great thing for the game. It shows a lot of courage not only to do the things that he's able to do, but also compete on the level he's competing on, and to be as successful as he is. I think he's going to be a *great* pitcher one day."

Reporter Dave Cunningham also liked what he saw. "I noticed that the first couple of times I saw him pitch in spring training," he said, "you watch how he switches the glove. He's so smooth that after a couple of innings of watching him for the very first time, all of a sudden, you're not paying attention to that — you're just watching the game. Which is exactly how he would prefer it."

Still, Jim was disappointed not to get a win for his new team. However, the baseball season is 162 games long, and he would have many more chances.

In Jim's second game, he faced the Oakland Athletics, the defending American League champions. And, much like his first game, Jim was the victim of poor defense by his teammates. He gave up four runs, but only two of them were earned, and the Angels lost, 5–0. Along with the errors, so far Jim's teammates weren't scoring any runs for him, either. But even though the crowd booed when the Angels made the errors, Jim knew that these things happen in baseball, and he was upset *for* his teammates, not *with* them.

Jim pitched six innings that day, giving up nine hits and two walks, but he also got his first four strikeouts. After two games, his earned run average stood at 4.24.

Mike Moore, the Oakland pitcher that day, was overpowering, and so after two starts in the big leagues, Jim was still looking for his first win.

Jim's next start was against the surprisingly good Baltimore Orioles. The season before, the Orioles had lost more than twenty games in a row to open the season; this season, however, they had started off with a victory over the Boston Red Sox and were still playing very well.

On this day, though, Jim was too good for the Orioles. He pitched six innings, giving up only two runs on four hits. He walked three batters — all of them in the third inning — and got one strikeout.

But the Orioles also stole several bases.

"One thing he does have to work on," Angel catcher Bill Schroeder said, "is his delivery to home plate with a runner on first base. They have a tendency to get a good jump on him, and it's difficult to throw runners out. They do steal more when he's out there, but you can't really do anything about that, at the expense of his stuff on the ball."

This is a problem that young pitchers often have. Many young pitchers deliver the ball to home plate with a very high leg kick. When they get to the major leagues, they have to learn what is called a slide step. A slide step is exactly what it sounds like: a pitcher *slides* his leg towards home plate, rather than using an exaggerated leg kick. Many pitchers find this hard to master and have to make the change gradually.

But when Jim left the game in the sixth inning, Greg Minton came in to relieve him, and then Bryan Harvey came in to save the game. The final score was the Angels 3, and the Orioles 2. Jim finally had his first big league victory.

"I think he's a good role model," Orioles relief pitcher Mark Williamson said. "He definitely belongs in the big leagues. I think that people are overdoing his handicap. I mean, look at him. He throws very hard, and he knows what he's doing out there. He's a pitcher; he's trying to beat us. And we're going to try and beat him."

Gregg Olson, Jim's former teammate — and roommate — from the Pan-American Games, was now playing for the Orioles, and he was very happy to see his friend in the big leagues, too. Gregg was also a rookie and had spent the 1988 season in the minor leagues.

"I was surprised when everybody was saying that he was going to go to Double-A, and then he made the team," Gregg said. "I was surprised because it's such a big jump." Gregg had made the jump from Double-A ball to the major leagues, and so he knew what he was talking about. "Jim's a great guy. I've been rooting for him."

Jim was very happy, too. He had his first official victory, and now he *really* felt like a major league baseball player.

8
Sliders and Strikeouts

One thing about major league baseball is that tomorrow is always another day, and there is always another game. So Jim didn't have very long to savor his first victory. The Angels were playing very well; the main competition in their division, the Oakland Athletics, had lost several players to injuries and were struggling a little; and Jim just wanted to help his team keep winning.

Five days after he beat Baltimore, Jim was on the mound again. This time, he would be facing the Toronto Blue Jays, who had drafted him back in high school when he decided to go to college instead. Jim wanted to pitch especially well. And he did.

It was a very exciting game, with the Angels

finally winning in the tenth inning on a Johnny Ray (the Angels' second baseman) sacrifice fly. Outfielder Dante Bichette scored the winning run. And although reliever Greg Minton had gotten the official victory, coming in to pitch in the ninth and tenth innings, Jim knew that he had done his share, too.

Jim's fastball was overpowering that night, and his slider was the best it had been all season. He gave up a home run to outfielder Jesse Barfield, but still pitched very well.

Jim's worst inning was the sixth. He gave up a single to 1987 American League Most Valuable Player George Bell, who promptly stole second. George took third when Jim threw a wild pitch. Nervous now, Jim balked and George was awarded home plate by the umpires.

Except for that run, and the Barfield homer, Jim had a superb game. He pitched eight innings, giving up nine — mostly scattered — hits. He didn't walk anyone, and even more importantly, he struck out nine Blue Jay batters, by far the most strikeouts he had had in any major league game so far.

Jim kept the score close — all a major league manager expects his starting pitchers to do — and then Greg Minton came in to finish and win the game. It was a big victory for the team, and a dramatic one.

Toronto All-Star shortstop Tony Fernández was

yet another American League player to be impressed by this rookie pitcher. "With just the one arm," he said, "you would think that he wouldn't be able to perform, but he has shown everybody that it doesn't matter. That no matter what kind of injury you have in your life, if you work hard to overcome it, you can." Tony also remarked that, the first time he faced Jim, he had a little bit of trouble picking up the ball in Jim's pitching delivery. "It was tougher for me to pick up the ball," he said. "Maybe because I was *looking* for the switch, to see how he does it, I didn't concentrate on his delivery point. But I guess the more you face him, the more you get used to it."

Baseball reporter Dave Cunningham agreed with that assessment. "As the season has gone on," he said, "I'm less and less aware of the fact that he has one hand. The only time you think about it is when there's a smash liner right back through the box that he's not quite ready for, and you think, What is that guy *doing* out there? But ninety-nine percent of the time, it never crosses your mind. But, hey, that's the way the ball comes off the bat at the major league level. Whether you've got one hand or two hands, sooner or later, it's going to hit you."

In fact, the joke that many baseball players and writers were repeating, about what Jim would do if a smash line drive headed right towards him, was that he would do what any other pitcher would do: *duck*. No one was quite sure who came up with this joke, but everyone seemed to agree with it. Baseball pitchers are, after all, often notoriously poor fielders. If anything, Jim is *better* at fielding than many other pitchers because he spends so much time working at it.

The baseball schedule being what it is, Jim's next game was also against Toronto. This time, the game was *at* Toronto, and this time, Jim got the win.

Jim set down the first nine batters he faced easily and pitched a total of six-and-a-third innings. (Each out counts for one third of an inning.) He gave up only four hits and two runs, and the Angels ended up with a 5–3 victory. Jim had four strikeouts, but he also walked four batters, and three bases were stolen against him. It was apparent that he still needed some practice holding runners on base. Along with developing the better curveball and change-up, this would be a long-term project. The important thing is that the Angels won again, and the team was playing good baseball.

Jim's next outing wasn't quite as good. In fact, it was his worst of the season, and he stayed in the game for only three innings. His opponents were the New York Yankees, a franchise with a long and famous history. That history may have made Jim a little nervous, because outfielder

Rickey Henderson started the game off with a double, and things didn't improve.

After Henderson scored in the first, the Yankees loaded the bases in the second, and scored again. Jesse Barfield, who had homered off Jim when playing for Toronto, had been traded to the Yankees. Facing Jim as a Yankee, he homered *again* in the third inning. Later in that same inning the Yankees got another home run, and that pretty much made it a day for Jim. He gave up five runs in three innings. He did have five strikeouts, but other than that, it was a game to forget.

Jim's next start also looked to be a challenging one. Not only would he be pitching against the heavy-hitting Boston Red Sox, but he would be going against two-time Cy Young Award-winner Roger Clemens.

Jim's teammates got him off to a good start by scoring a surprising five runs off Clemens in the very first inning, highlighted by catcher Lance Parrish's two-run homer. Now, it was up to Jim to take it from there, and that is exactly what he did. Amazingly, Roger Clemens had been knocked out of the game by the third inning, and it was Jim — the rookie — who pitched a brilliant game.

He pitched the full nine innings — for his first complete game as a professional — and limited the Red Sox to four singles. Wade Boggs and Marty Barrett each had one, and Mike Greenwell had two. Jim walked two batters, but he also caused the Red Sox to hit into four double plays, so he faced only thirty batters in the whole game. The minimum number of batters a pitcher can face — if he pitches a *perfect* game — is twenty-seven, and Jim pitched to only thirty.

It was quite a game. The Red Sox were unable to score any runs, so not only did Jim have his first complete game, but he had his first major league shutout. On top of that, he had beaten Roger Clemens, one of the best pitchers in baseball today. There was no question that this game was the highlight of Jim's season so far.

"Most people have, maybe, a thousand innings in the minor leagues before they ever get here, and he has none at all," Angels' pitching coach Marcel Lachemann said. "It makes what he has accomplished so far all the more impressive. He has a great deal of poise, and he's obviously got a great deal of ability. He's learning how to pitch in the big leagues, and that's tough to do."

The Red Sox had also become members of the Jim Abbott admiration club.

"He's an outstanding pitcher, from what I've seen so far," Dwight Evans, the Red Sox right fielder since 1974, said. "I'm surprised that he has the control that he has, and the knowledge of pitching that he has, at such an early age. He throws hard, and he's not afraid to come inside. He does things with the ball that a lot of people *don't* do. And that's the secret, really, to pitching — knowing what to do at certain times. He's had Lance Parrish, who's a seasoned veteran, behind the plate for him, and what Parrish is calling, and where he's putting his glove — this kid's throwing to it. I give him [Jim] a lot of credit."

Second baseman Marty Barrett echoed these thoughts. "You know, a lot of left-handed pitchers are afraid to pitch inside," he said thoughtfully, "and they get hurt that way. But he's learned to do it, and he has good movement on all of his pitches. If he keeps throwing the way he does, he's going to have a long and fulfilling career."

The Red Sox star center fielder, Ellis Burks, was another player who agreed that Jim was a very good pitcher. He was particularly impressed that Jim had held the Red Sox to so few hits. "With a club like us," Ellis said, "where we have a lot of free swingers, and a lot of guys hitting .300 or pretty close, that's amazing. He's effective and he's smart. He keeps the ball inside when he needs to, and away when he has to do that. You can't really look for one pitch because he has an excellent slider, *and* he has a good fastball."

Since Jim had pitched a shutout against Roger Clemens, maybe now the press would write about him as a *pitcher*, rather than as a pitcher with a handicap.

"He told me once," reporter Dave Cunningham said, "that he kind of dreams of waking up in the morning, getting the paper, and reading a whole story about a game he pitched with no reference at all to the fact that he was born with one hand. It'll happen — if it hasn't already."

Pitching games like the one against the Red Sox was a very good way to speed up that process. And Jim's next game was going to be against the Yankees. A rematch.

9
Ups and Downs

Jim's first start against the Yankees, only about ten days earlier, hadn't been very successful, and he wanted this one to be different. This time, though, instead of pitching in friendly Anaheim Stadium, he was pitching in Yankee Stadium. Yankee Stadium, with its long row of retired numbers on the fence in deep center field — numbers that had belonged to players like Babe Ruth and Lou Gehrig — can be a very intimidating place to pitch. Yankee Stadium can be intimidating for the *home* team, let alone the visiting team.

Judging from Jim's pitching that night, he wasn't very nervous. It was a long game, about four hours, and the Angels came out on top. Jim got the victory, with Greg Minton notching the save. It was Jim's fourth victory of the season, and

Greg's fifth save. (Although the rule can be complicated, basically a pitcher gets a save when he enters the game with his team already leading, and manages to preserve that win.)

Jim pitched five-and-a-third innings of four-run ball, with relievers Bob McClure, Dan Petry, and finally, Greg Minton coming in to finish the game. Jim gave up ten hits, with three walks and two strikeouts. When Jim left the game in the sixth inning, with the Angels leading 6–4, the Yankee fans gave him a standing ovation. Since the Yankee fans are famous for avid Yankee partisanship, this was a very special tribute, indeed. Now, Jim's pitching record for the season was a more than respectable four wins against three defeats. After losing to the Yankees in his first start against them, it was a relief for Jim to get the win this time.

Jim's final May start was in Milwaukee. He pitched well, but it was a very tense game. Angel teammate Claudell Washington hit a home run and then, the next time he came to the plate, the Milwaukee pitcher threw a pitch very close to his head. This is a good way to start a fight in baseball. In fact, it is the *best* way to start one.

Later in the game, Jim hit Milwaukee batter Gus Polidor with a pitch. By accident? No one really knew, but both benches cleared, there was a lot of pushing and shoving, and the umpires warned both teams not to escalate the tension anymore.

Throwing at batters is a controversial, and unspoken, tradition in baseball. If one team's pitcher throws at a hitter, the other team's pitcher is expected to retaliate. This usually goes on until a shoving match breaks out. Unlike hockey, baseball players rarely throw actual punches.

It is considered fair to throw close to a batter as long as the pitcher keeps the ball low. Any pitch thrown near a batter's head can result in a pitcher being thrown out of the game, or even suspended. Since the designated hitter rule went into effect in the American League, more close pitches are thrown, since pitchers don't have to worry about batting themselves and risk having the ball thrown at them in retaliation. The designated hitter rule is not used in the National League, so fewer close pitches are thrown there.

There are several slang terms used to describe a close pitch. It can be called a "brushback pitch," a "knockdown pitch," "buzzing the hitter," and "chin music." Like most baseball terms, these phrases are both colorful and descriptive. In many leagues a pitcher who throws a pitch at someone intentionally has a very good chance of getting kicked out of that league permanently. It could even happen in the big leagues, but it is hard to prove that a pitcher threw wildly intentionally since many pitchers throw wildly whether they want to or not. Either way, it is a dangerous thing to do, and umpires always firmly discourage the practice.

Once all the excitement died down, Jim's game against Milwaukee was a close one. He pitched seven innings, with only two hits and two runs. He walked three batters, but got six others to strike out.

In the eighth inning, Jim walked the first two batters, and with a narrow 3–2 Angel lead, he was taken out of the game. The Angels ended up winning by that same score, and Jim's record had improved to five and three.

But after that game, Jim felt tightness and pain in his pitching shoulder. The Angels' team doctor diagnosed Jim's problem as tendinitis and ordered him to rest his arm for almost two weeks. Athletes often get tendinitis. Pitchers are very prone to this, particularly in their elbow and shoulder muscles. The muscles and tendons get inflamed from the constant use — and abuse — that they are given. This is not a very serious injury, but the only cure is rest. An athlete who doesn't rest risks making the inflammation much worse, and maybe even tearing or rupturing one of the muscles.

"It's a big adjustment for Jim this year because normally he wouldn't be throwing this much," Angel catcher Bill Schroeder said. "His season would be over by now. When you go from a college season of forty games to a major league season of 162 games, it's kind of a shock to your system."

It was frustrating to wait for his arm to heal, but Jim knew that it was the only sensible thing to do. It was much better to miss a start or two *now*, than to make the injury worse, and maybe be out of action even longer.

Jim did have to miss a start, but he felt better by the time his next turn came around — against the Kansas City Royals. The Angels were slumping a little, and Jim wanted to help them get back on the winning track. Unfortunately it didn't work out that way.

Jim was happy to find that his shoulder felt much better, and that he could pitch without pain, but his team lost the game. Jim pitched well for the first five innings, but then fell apart in the sixth. He ended up letting four runs come across the plate and was taken out of the game. There was only one out when he left.

So, in five-and-a-third innings, Jim was charged with four runs, on six hits and three walks. He also had two strikeouts. The Angels were able to score only three runs of their own, and ended up losing the game by a score of 5–3. Jim's record fell to five wins and four losses. But at least his arm felt healthy again, and Jim knew that he would just have to go out and try again next time.

That next start was to be against the Detroit Tigers, the team Jim had rooted for while growing up in Flint, Michigan. His favorite team. It would be strange to be on the mound against them. It was also strange — and exciting — to be on the same field *with* them.

The game was in Detroit, at Tiger Stadium, and about sixty of Jim's relatives and friends, including his parents and grandfather, were able to come. For most of them, it was the first time they had ever been able to see Jim pitch professionally in person.

Knowing that so many people he cared about were in the stands watching, Jim was a little nervous at the beginning of the game. Tiger outfielder Gary Ward hit a home run in the first inning, and after that, Jim knew that he would have to concentrate harder. Working to forget the crowd and the excitement of pitching in the stadium where he had watched games growing up, Jim focused on the job at hand.

And his teammates helped make the job easier. Outfielder Claudell Washington hit a three-run homer, and outfielder Chili Davis and first baseman Wally Joyner chipped in with runs batted in of their own, giving Jim a lead to protect.

Jim pitched seven innings. The Tigers scored three runs on nine hits, but the most important number was the final score. The Angels 6, the Tigers 3.

Jim had come home with a victory. And his friends and family were all there to see it.

10
National Television

Jim's next game was against the Baltimore Orioles. It was also the Thursday night Game of the Week, and the first time Jim had pitched on national television since the Olympics.

The game did not start well for Jim. He had two strikes on the first batter, Mike Devereaux, but then hit him on the foot with a pitch he was trying to throw for a ball. So Devereaux went to first. Then Jim walked Phil Bradley and Cal Ripkin, and the bases were loaded with nobody out. Angel catcher Lance Parrish and pitching coach Marcel Lachemann went out to talk to Jim, to calm him down, and Jim got the next batter to hit a grounder to third. Third baseman Jack Howell threw the ball home for the force, and there was one out.

The next batter hit a grounder to first base, but

Wally Joyner was only able to get the out at first, and a run scored. Then, Baltimore catcher Bob Melvin hit a shot right up the middle, and Jim wasn't able to switch his glove in time to catch it. *Two* runs scored. Jim got out of the inning when the next batter hit a fly ball to Claudell Washington in right field, but the Angels were now losing 3–0.

Jim had a better second inning, getting two of the batters to strike out, but he gave up another run in the third. When he was taken out of the game after pitching four innings, he had given up five runs on only three hits. But he had been hurt by the four batters he walked, three of whom scored.

The Angels had not been playing well lately, and although they came back to score five runs of their own, it was a case of too little too late as the Orioles got a home run to win 6–5. The Angels were now in third place in the Western Division, behind the Oakland A's and the Kansas City Royals. The team needed to start winning again.

Jim's next game was one of the most disappointing of his season because he pitched very well, but the team still lost a close one. Their opponents were the Cleveland Indians. Although it has been many years since Cleveland has even come close to winning a pennant, they are a team with a lot of good, young players. Out on the mound, Jim just wanted to stop them.

He pitched an excellent game, but his opponent, Scott Bailes, did, too. In seven-and-two-thirds innings, Jim gave up only four hits. He had three walks and three strikeouts. Of the ninety-four pitches he threw, sixty-three of them were strikes, which is considered a very good ratio.

In the eighth inning, Jim got two outs, but he also had runners on second and third. Angel manager Doug Rader decided that, with the score tied 1–1, he would bring in a relief pitcher. Ace reliever Greg Minton had gotten hurt and was on the disabled list, so Rader brought in Willie Fraser. Unfortunately Willie threw a wild pitch, and the go-ahead run came in from third.

The Angels were unable to score in the ninth inning, and lost the game 2–1. It was a heartbreaking loss for Jim and his teammates. It is sad to lose any close game, but losing it in the late innings is even more depressing.

The Cleveland Indian players, like other teams before them, noticed Jim's poise and maturity on the field.

"I don't think of him as being handicapped," Indian slugger Joe Carter said, during an interview. "He's got his left arm and that's all that matters because that's the one he throws with. It kind of amazes you, on a ground ball back to the mound, when he does his little motion." Joe demonstrated the glove switch with his own hands, and shook his head with admiration. "I guess he's learned to adjust since day one, and it's a natural motion to him." Then Joe grinned. "We may seem a little different to *him* because we don't do things the way he does."

"It's just phenomenal that he's overcome such a disability, and made it to the big leagues," Indian third baseman Brook Jacoby said. "It shows youngsters that no matter what kind of problems you have, if you work hard enough, you can achieve your goals."

First baseman Pete O'Brien was just as enthusiastic. "He's spent a lot of years working, and it shows," Pete said. "He's just an outstanding pitcher. You've had a handful of rookies who have come on, and made an impact like he has, but not too many. I think, emotionally, he's probably as stable a rookie as you'll find. He's that much more ahead of the game, I think, when it comes to dealing with certain pressures baseball has." Pete also thought that Jim's pitching motion was very good. "He's got a ball that's very tough to pick up. He's got a good delivery — it's a little deceptive, and you're not picking the ball up very easily — but I think that's just his motion. I don't think it has anything to do with his disability. And he's very quick in the exchange with his glove. . . ."

Jim was happy that he had pitched well that night, but he would have been much happier if his team had come out on top.

11
Rookie Record

As the mid-season All-Star break came closer, the Angels were starting to get hot. And Oakland was starting to slump. The Angels needed to take advantage of this situation.

Jim would have two more starts before the All-Star break, and he wanted to make the most of them. First, he would go against the Texas Rangers. The Rangers had made a lot of trades during the off-season, and had been expected to be a serious threat in the pennant race. But after starting the season with a long string of victories, the Rangers had faded. Even so, they were a dangerous team, with a very potent lineup.

Jim felt the pressure that night since he hadn't won a game in over two weeks. On this night, teammates Wally Joyner, Lance Parrish, and

Glenn Hoffmann each had two hits, and the Angels scored five runs for him.

In return, Jim pitched eight strong innings. He held the Rangers to five hits, including a double by Ranger left fielder Pete Incaviglia. Jim and Pete were the only two rookies to have made the jump from amateur baseball to the big leagues during the eighties.

The Rangers scored two runs on those five hits, but that wasn't enough to catch the Angels. In fact, the Rangers would only have scored one run, but Jim balked a second run home in the eighth inning. However, he walked only one batter — much better than he'd been doing in his last couple of starts — and he got six strikeouts. Ranger second baseman Jeff Kunkel accounted for three of these strikeouts, fanning every time he came to the plate.

Manager Rader took Jim out after the eighth inning, and brought in Bryan Harvey to finish the game. Bryan gave up a hit and a walk in the ninth, but kept the Rangers from scoring, giving Jim his seventh win.

And that seventh win set a rookie record. Among the ten pitchers who had started their careers by jumping directly to the major leagues, Dick Ruthven had posted the most victories in his first season.

Jim, who was now seven and five, had set a new record for victories in less than half a season. There was no question that the Angels had made the right decision by having Jim bypass the minors.

Jim's final start before the All-Star break was against the Minnesota Twins. The Twins are a very good hitting team, usually placing second behind the Boston Red Sox in team batting average. The Twins won the World Series back in 1987, and are still a solid team. Kirby Puckett — considered by many baseball observers to be the best player in the game today — is the Twins' center fielder, and the Twins have a lot of other talented players, including All-Star third baseman Gary Gaetti, big first baseman Kent Hrbek, and outfielder Dan Gladden.

But the Angels had been playing very well lately, and a victory by Jim against the Twins would guarantee that his team would go into the All-Star break in first place in the Western Division.

Pitching carefully, Jim gave up a lot of hits — nine — but the Twins didn't manage to score until Twins' catcher Brian Harper singled in the seventh to drive in Minnesota's first — and only — run of the game. Jim struck out seven, including both Kirby Puckett and Kent Hrbek, once apiece. Again, his control was very good, and he walked only one batter.

Manager Rader took Jim out after Brian Harper's single, and reliever Greg Minton came in to finish the seventh, and pitch the eighth. Minton held the Twins scoreless, and then Bryan Harvey pitched a perfect ninth inning, earning his twelfth save of the season. Jim was credited with his eighth victory.

Angel catcher Lance Parrish had a big day, hitting a two-run homer, and Wally Joyner and Johnny Ray each drove in runs.

It was a team effort, and because of that effort, the Angels would finish the first half of the season in first place. Exactly, of course, where they wanted to be. With half a season to go, anything could happen, but it looked like the Angels would have a good chance to go to the play-offs, maybe even the World Series. Jim was glad that, so far, he had been able to contribute. He could hardly wait for the second half of the season to begin.

12
A Very Bright Future

Athough Jim wasn't quite as successful during the second half of the season, he will be able to look back at what he has accomplished and feel proud. Of course, in all sports there are highs and lows, but so far Jim has made a very good beginning.

Jim's teammates were also excited by his performance.

"I think he's handled all the attention that he's had very well," catcher Bill Schroeder said. "Especially for a rookie. Everybody talks about the handicap, but around here, we don't consider him to have any problem like that. It's never discussed, it's never thought of."

Outfielder Devon White seconded this opinion. "He has a great arm," Devon said, "and, you know, with the loss of his hand — we don't look at it like that, and a lot of major leaguers have stopped looking at it like that. He's normal as far as we're concerned. His attitude is the greatest."

Without a doubt, the constant media attention had put a lot of pressure on Jim, and it is amazing that he was able to produce as well as he did, not allowing himself to be distracted. Many players would have had trouble coping with the situation.

"He's heard so many questions," reporter Dave Cunningham said. "The same questions, over and over again. The thing that's remarkable is that he is so poised, and so together. He handles it all so well. Just — unflustered. But he wants the attention for what he does on the field; he doesn't want the attention because he doesn't have a right hand. For a rookie, he's done amazingly well, and I think he'll only get better."

The publicity is the big difference between Jim and the average rookie. Most rookies would have the freedom to make a gradual adjustment to life in the big leagues. Most rookies are not the top story on the sports news every single time they go out onto the field. Most rookies probably would not be able to handle it.

"He has more publicity attention than anyone on our ball club," pitching coach Marcel Lachemann observed, "and we've got a lot of veteran players — we've got a couple of guys who'll probably be in the Hall of Fame. Jim is well accepted by the rest of the guys because he's not overly impressed by himself. He realizes that he's got a lot to learn, and he appreciates everybody trying to help him. Blyleven, Finley, the rest of the pitchers — they've all helped him. The catchers have, too." Then Marcel smiled. "He's been a refreshing kid to have because he has a lot of enthusiasm, but he also has a great deal of ability. It's been fun."

Catcher Bill Schroeder, who — along with Lance Parrish — had probably spent more time working with Jim than anyone other than Marcel Lachemann, agreed completely.

"His progress from the beginning of the year until now [the All-Star break] has been dramatic," Bill said. "He's never failed at anything he's tried to do, and he's going to keep improving. He works hard, and he takes it seriously."

This isn't to say that Jim is all work and no play. When asked what was his favorite thing to do — other than baseball — with his free time, Jim thought for a minute.

"Well, I like to sit around and listen to music," he said. "Just relax, get away from the game." He shook his head when asked if he liked one particular *type* of music. "Any kind — I go in streaks. It just depends on the mood I'm in."

Jim, like most people his age — and size — also enjoys eating. "I like chicken a lot," he said, and grinned. "And seafood. I like seafood quite a bit. Chinese food. Pizza." Then he shrugged, indicating that he liked *most* food. And considering that Jim is six feet, three inches tall and in very good shape, he can eat just about anything he wants. Whenever he wants.

But Jim's mind is never far from baseball. An athlete can always improve, and Jim has several clear goals, which the Angels' coaches and players will help him achieve. For one, he needs a more effective and consistent curveball to go with his already terrific fastball and slider. It would also help him as a pitcher if he could develop a dependable change-up pitch. Change-ups are a particularly good weapon for a fastball pitcher because they throw off the hitter's timing so much. A good change-up makes a good fastball look even faster. Maybe the most important thing will be for Jim to work on his pitching delivery when there are runners on base. Although the catcher generally gets the blame, base runners usually steal bases off the *pitcher*. A catcher can only throw the ball once he gets it, so pitchers have to work on speeding up their motion to the plate.

To some degree, Jim may also work to improve his control. A pitcher needs to be able to throw a strike when he needs a strike, but he never wants the batter to feel too confident. The confrontation between pitcher and batter is one of the most exciting in sports, and each wants to intimidate the other. A good hitter will always stand as close to the plate as possible, so that he can cover more of the strike zone with the "fat" part of the bat. A good pitcher needs to be able to throw the ball inside, and make the hitter back away. A smart pitcher will usually follow an inside pitch with an outside pitch that the batter will then miss. On the other hand, the batter *expects* the pitcher to turn around and throw an outside pitch, so he'll be waiting for that. Therefore, an even *smarter* pitcher might turn around and decide to surprise the batter by throwing another inside pitch, while the batter is leaning forward, looking for the outside pitch — that is why the pitcher-batter confrontation is so exciting. Jim is a very smart pitcher, and he enjoys this competition very much. Each player is trying to outwit the other, and there can be only one winner in each confrontation. One of the beauties of baseball is that — unlike most other sports — there can never be a tie. Someone always loses. Someone always wins.

As far as throwing to the inside part of the plate is concerned, most batters who have faced Jim Abbott would agree that Jim usually wins *that* battle.

The longer Jim is in the big leagues, the better he will become. He will learn more about each hitter he faces, discovering the pitches each batter can, and cannot, hit. A veteran pitcher is often able to prolong his career even after his fastball slows down simply because he has learned so much about *where* and *when* to throw the ball. A pitcher's development is always fun to watch, and at this stage, it's a pretty good bet that Jim can become one of the better pitchers in the American League.

Gradually the stories about Jim's "handicap" will go away, and the stories will be about Jim's pitching. Period. Jim probably looks forward to that day more than anything (except, maybe, a chance to pitch for his team in a World Series).

No matter what happens — no matter what Jim does, or doesn't accomplish during the rest of his pitching career, his story will always be an inspiration to people who want to do something that they aren't sure they can do. Jim is *proof* that, with hard work and determination, people can overcome incredible odds.

"Jimmy's a class guy," said Angel infielder Glenn Hoffmann — who had to overcome a cardiac problem of his own. "I think the adversity he's come through made him a better person. I think that he'll have a lot of influence on kids, and hopefully, he'll steer them in the right direction."

"He's great," teammate Kent Anderson agreed. "I've only known him for a short while, but everything I'd have to say about him would be good."

Fellow Angel rookie Bob Rose, an infielder who came up to the majors for the first time during the season, also raved about Jim. "He's one of a kind," Bob said. "It's just — it's unreal what he can do. He's awesome."

It doesn't seem to matter who is asked — teammates, coaches, opposing players — everybody has something nice to say about Jim Abbott.

Almost everybody.

"Well, *I* don't like him," first baseman Wally Joyner teased, and laughed.

Pitcher Kirk McCaskill laughed, and agreed. "I don't have *anything* nice to say about that guy."

Then both players got more serious.

"Jimmy's a great inspiration to a lot of people, including me," Wally said, no longer joking. "When somebody has that much desire, it gives you inspiration about a lot of things. It shows that anything you want, you can achieve. So he's given me a few thoughts about life, and principles of living. I've enjoyed having him on the ball club." Then Wally smiled. "I mean, getting here and achieving your dream — that's what it's all about."

But Kirk may have put it best. "There's nothing really original you can say about Jim, because everyone thinks the same thing about him — he's an amazing story," he said. "I'm just glad I've had the opportunity to play with him, and get to know him."

Above and beyond what Jim has achieved on the baseball field, the most amazing thing about him just might be that he *is* so nice. Jim is a *good* person. In recent years, far too many of America's heroes have disappointed their fans. Being a hero is a responsibility, and Jim has always handled that responsibility with respect and dignity. He is a *true* American hero.

When asked what is the best thing about being in the big leagues, Jim smiled.

"The best thing is just making it, you know?" he

said. "Doing something that you always wanted to do. To be here sometimes, in your first year, you still look back and say, well, you know, I'm here, and this is *really* something. You never outgrow it. The team has been good to me, and it's really been an enjoyable year. I'm very fortunate."

Anyone who is a baseball fan and has followed Jim's career is fortunate.

Jim Abbott *is* one-of-a-kind. And professional baseball is lucky to have him.

Jim Abbott's Awards and Honors

1985
March of Dimes Amateur Athlete of the Year

1986
Most Courageous Athlete, selected by the Philadelphia Sportswriters Association
Big Ten Play-offs All-Tournament team

1987
The Golden Spikes Award, selected by the United States Baseball Federation
All-America, third team
All-Big Ten Conference, second team
ESPN Amateur Athlete of the Week
Big Ten Play-offs All-Tournament team
Member, Team USA, silver medal, Pan-American Games
Academy Awards of Sport, Award for Courage

1988

Eighth overall selection in the major league baseball free-agent draft by the California Angels

Member, United States Olympic Baseball team, gold medal

Athlete of the Year for baseball, selected by the U.S. Olympic Committee

The Sullivan Award, selected by the AAU; first baseball player to ever win

All-Tournament team, World Baseball Championships, Parma, Italy

Big Ten Conference Player of the Year

All-Big Ten Conference, first team

Big Ten Play-offs All-Tournament team

The Sporting News All-America College Baseball team

March of Dimes Amateur Athlete of the Year

Tanqueray Achievement Award, for amateur sports

Big Ten-Jesse Owens Male Athlete of the Year

Baseball America All-America team, pre-season

Collegiate Baseball All-America team, pre-season

1989

Only the fifteenth player in the history of the amateur baseball draft to go directly to the major leagues

Won twelve games in his rookie season, a major league record for rookies

Step Back in Time with
SCHOLASTIC BIOGRAPHY